This Notebook Belongs To:

Miss Emma Johstone

Printed in Great Britain
by Amazon

25280047R00057